The "True Book" series is prepared
under the direction of
Illa Podendorf
Laboratory School, University of Chicago
Ninety-eight per cent of the text is in words from
the Combined Word List for Primary Reading

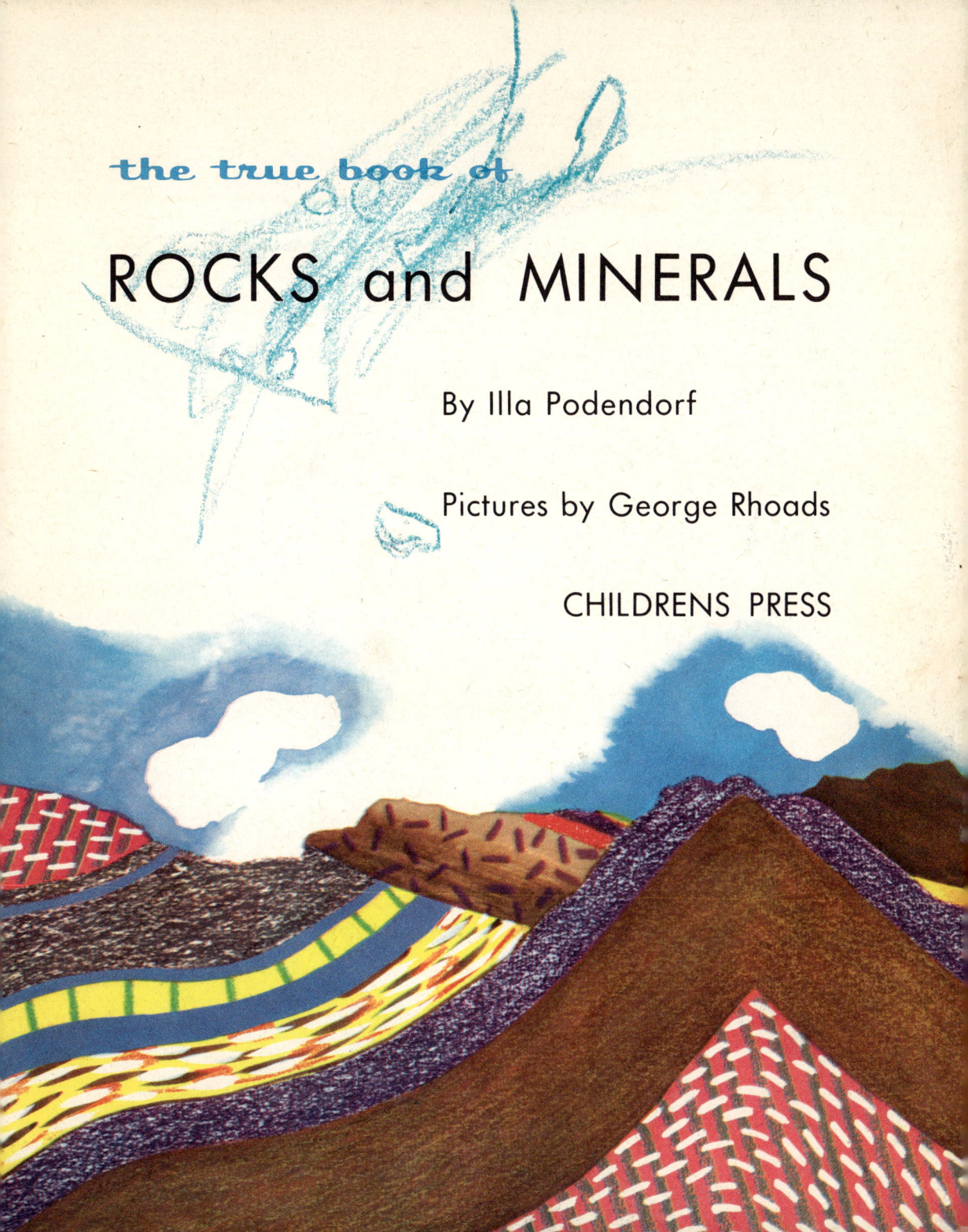

TABLE OF

Rocks are big and little, 6

Some rocks are made by fire, 12

Some rocks are made under water, 19

Some rocks are made from other rocks, 28

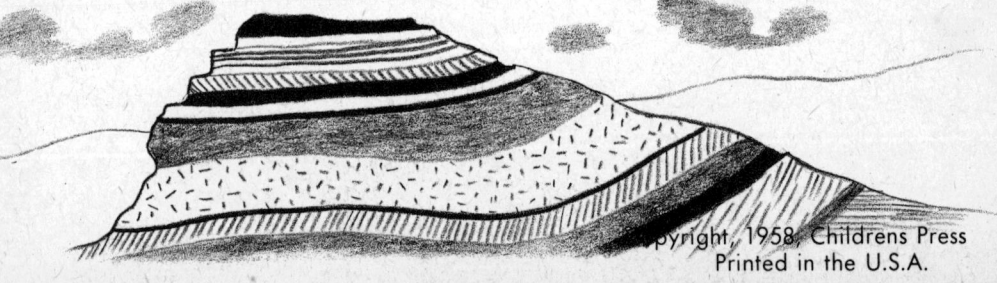

Copyright, 1958, Childrens Press
Printed in the U.S.A.

CONTENTS

Rocks are made from minerals, 33

Rocks tell stories of long ago, 40

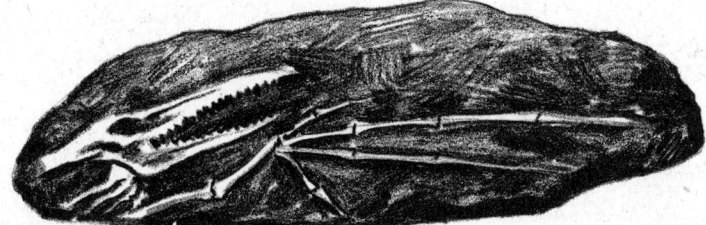

Scientists name rocks, 44

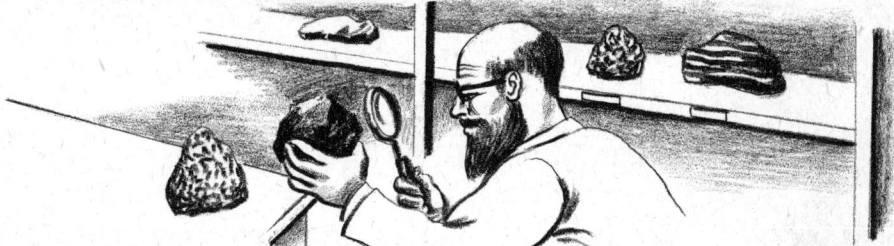

Important things to know about rocks, 48

ROCKS ARE BIG AND LITTLE

Some rocks are big.
Big rocks are called boulders.

Some rocks are small.
Small rocks are broken
from big rocks.

Some rocks are rough. Rough rocks may be made smooth by rolling around on the ground among other rocks.

Rough rocks may be made
smooth by rolling around
in water, too.

GRAY GRANITE

    Rocks are of many different kinds and colors.
    Granite is one kind of rock.
    Not all granite is the same color.

RED GRANITE

PINK GRANITE

SOME ROCKS ARE MADE BY FIRE

Fire-made rocks are called *igneous* rocks. Granite is a kind of fire-made rock. It is always made under the ground. It is a good building stone.

DIORITE

GABBRO

SYENITE

All these rocks were made by fire. They were all made under ground.

Not all fire-made rocks are made under ground. Some fire-made rocks are made from melted rock that is shot out of a volcano.

Melted rock cools quickly as it is shot out of a volcano. Even the foam from the melted rock cools and forms rocks. Pumice is a kind of rock which is made from foam.

PUMICE

Pumice does not weigh much. It has air spaces in it. It will float on water. Pumice is useful. It is sometimes used to polish other rocks.

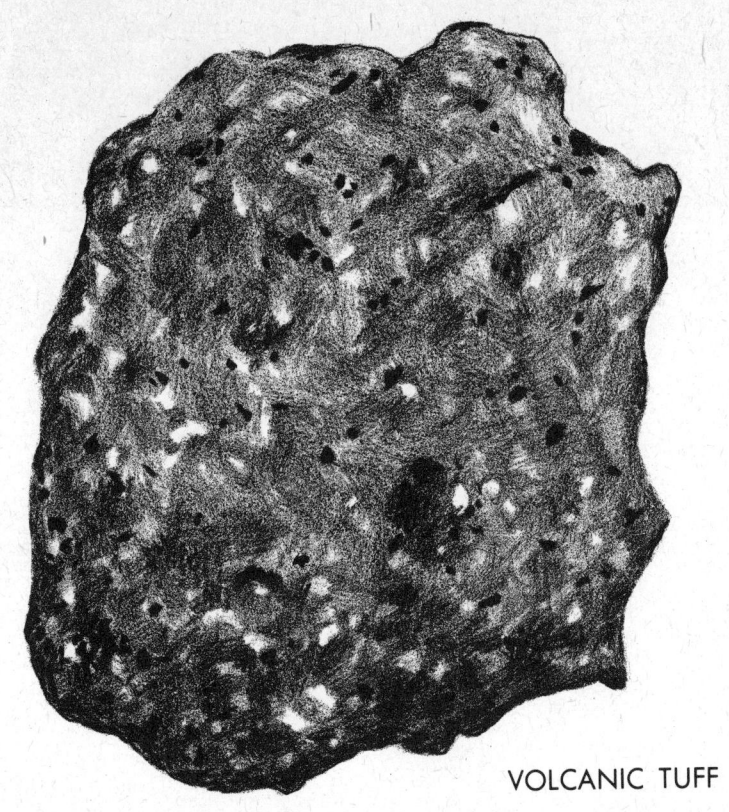

VOLCANIC TUFF

Some melted rock hardens into a kind of rock which is called volcanic tuff.

Volcanic tuff is heavier than pumice. It will not float.

BLACK OBSIDIAN

GREEN OBSIDIAN

Obsidian comes from volcanoes, too. It is sometimes called volcanic glass. It is shiny.

Basalt rocks are igneous rocks. Great walls are made of basalt rocks.

BASALT

18

SOME ROCKS ARE MADE UNDER WATER

Some kinds of rocks are not made from melted rock.

Some rocks are made under water. They are made from small pieces of shell and sand which gather there. They are called *sedimentary* rocks.

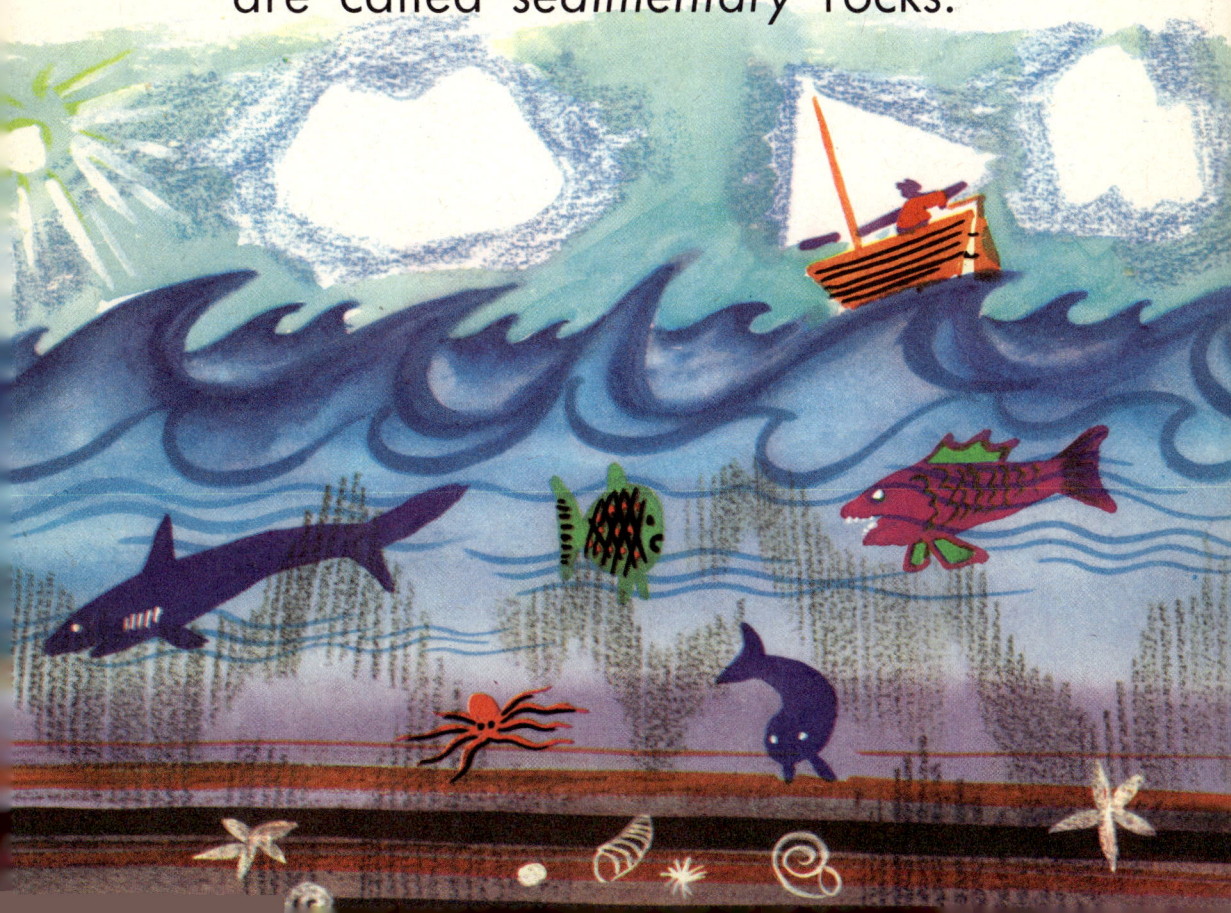

All these rocks are limestone.

GRAY LIMESTONE

CHALK (WHITE) LIMESTONE

VARIEGATED LIMESTONE

COQUINA LIMESTONE

They are sedimentary rocks.
It is easy to see shells
in this piece of limestone.

LITHOGRAPHIC STONE

When limestone is older and smoother, it is not so easy to see the shells. This kind of limestone is smooth enough to write on.

It takes many thousands of years for limestone to be made. Limestone is useful.

It is used for building buildings.

YELLOW, RED, GRAY SANDSTONE

Sandstone is made under water. It is made of grains of sand. Sandstone is not always the same color.

Conglomerate is made under water. It is made of little stones or pebbles held together by limestone.

CONGLOMERATE

Shale is made under water. It is made of mud. It smells muddy when it is wet. It is many different colors.

It scratches easily.

SHALE

SHALE

Water helps make agate, too.
People polish agate and make
things from it.

AGATE

SOME ROCKS ARE MADE FROM OTHER ROCKS

Rocks which are made from other rocks are called *metamorphic* rocks. There are many kinds of metamorphic rocks. The heat of the earth and the weight of the many layers of rocks on top of rocks help to cause them to change to kinds of metamorphic rocks. Slate is made from shale.

RED SLATE BLACK SLATE

Slate is harder than shale. It will not scratch so easily. Schist is made from conglomerate. It is many different colors.

SCHIST
(various forms)

WHITE, PINK, GREEN MARBLE

Marble is made from limestone. Marble is many different colors.

Marble can be made very smooth and shiny. Pretty things are made of it.

GNEISS

Gneiss may be made from granite. It has bands or streaks in it.

ROCKS ARE MADE FROM MINERALS

There are many kinds of minerals. Some rocks have more than one kind of mineral in them. Some rocks have only one kind of mineral in them. Talc is a mineral.

A talc rock scratches very easily. It feels smooth.

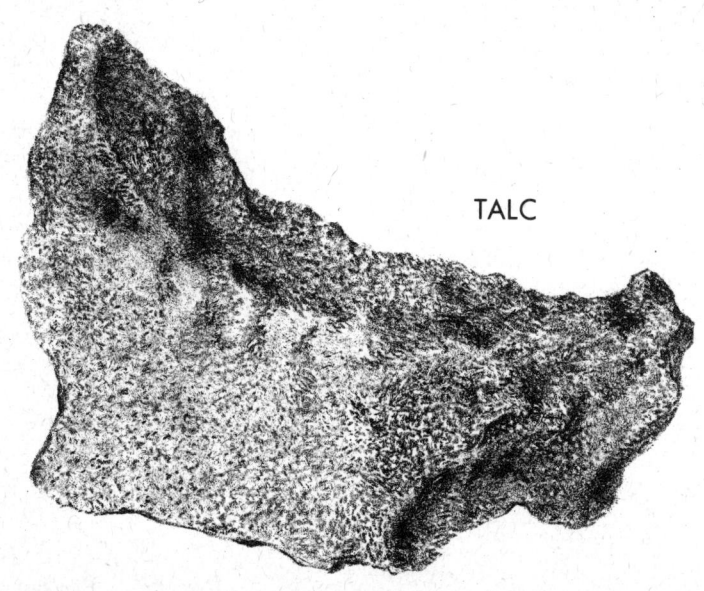
TALC

QUARTZ

    Quartz is a mineral. It is very hard. It is hard to scratch quartz.

    Sometimes minerals are crystals. Crystals are clear and have a certain shape. Quartz crystals always have six sides. Jewelry is often made of quartz crystals.

QUARTZ ROCK   POLISHED CRYSTAL   CRYSTAL

All these rocks are quartz.
But not all of them are crystals.
Sometimes several crystals
have been melted and hardened
in one piece. Then they are
no longer crystals.

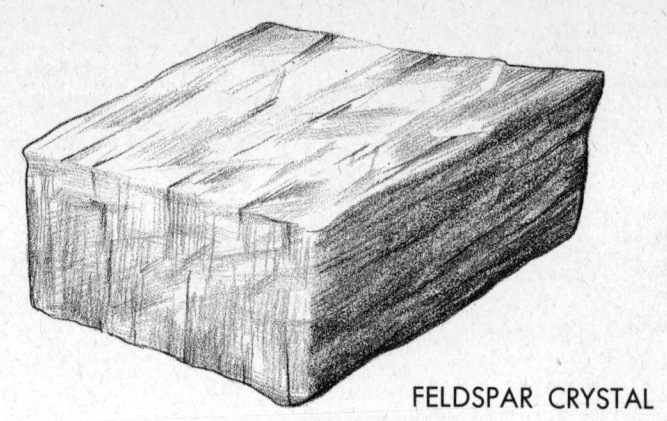

FELDSPAR CRYSTAL

Feldspar crystals always have four sides. Not all feldspar is in crystals.

NON-CRYSTAL FELDSPAR

CALCITE

CALCITE CRYSTAL

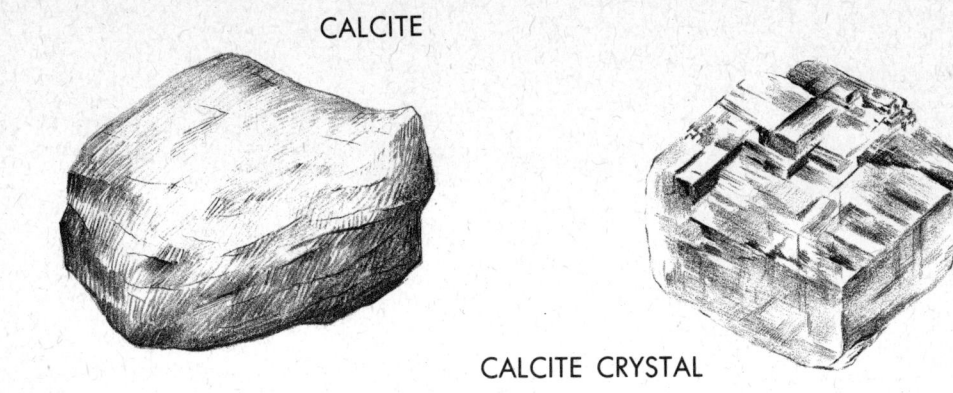

Calcite crystals make marks look double. Not all calcite is in crystals.

Mica is made of many thin sheets.

It is easy to see through one of the sheets.

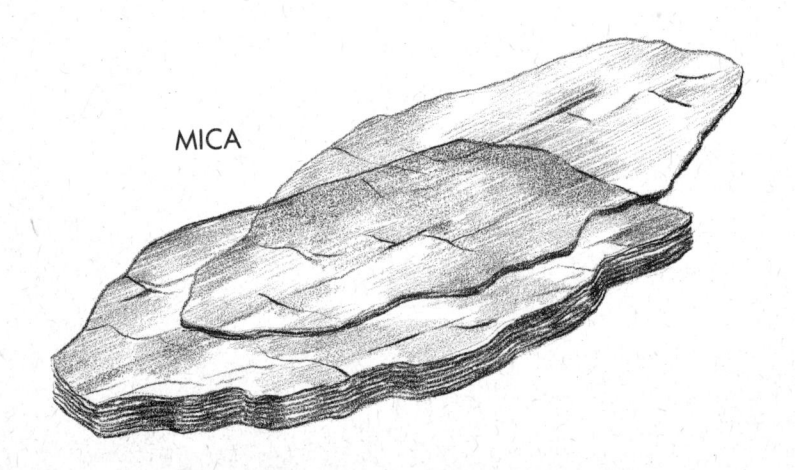

MICA

It is easy to see the crystals in some kinds of rocks. Granite is sure to have crystals of quartz, feldspar and mica in it. It is the crystals which make granite look speckled.

CRYSTALS IN GRANITE

ROCKS TELL STORIES OF LONG AGO

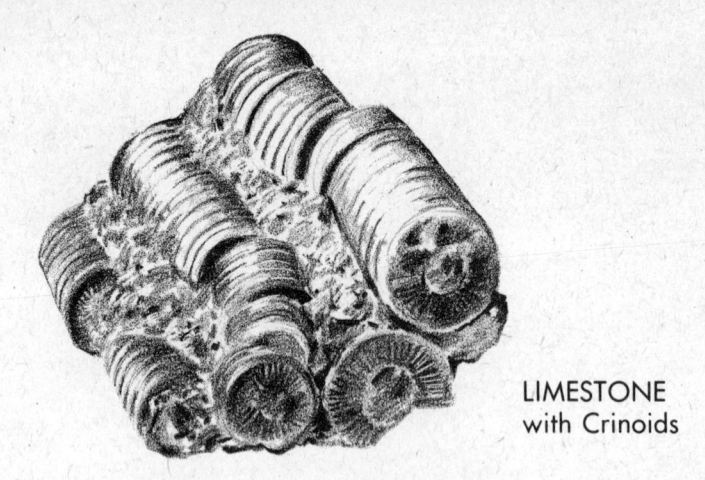

LIMESTONE
with Crinoids

Some rocks tell stories because they have prints of plants or animals in them. The prints are called fossils.

It takes many thousands of years for a rock to be made.

The plants and animals which are pictured in rocks lived many thousands of years ago.

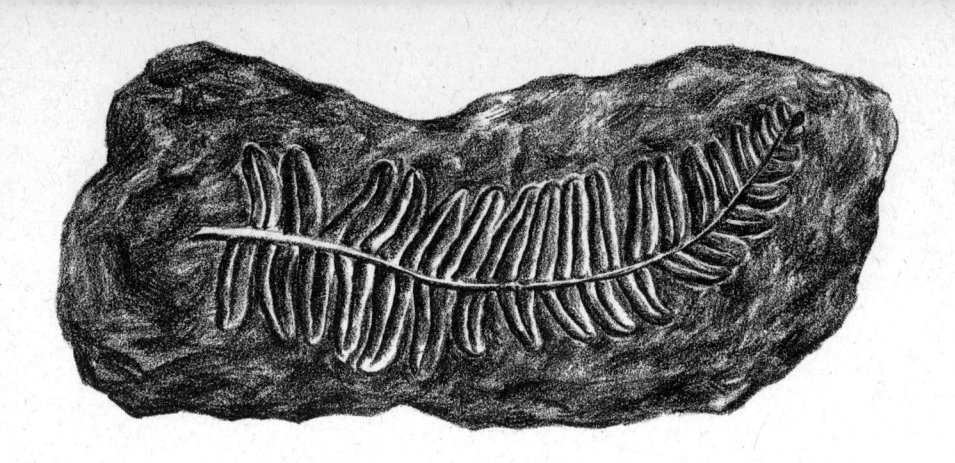

Fossils are usually found in limestone. This piece of limestone has a fossil of a leaf in it.

This piece of limestone has a fossil of a snail in it.

This piece of limestone has a part of an animal in it. The animal part has turned to stone and is a fossil.

This rock has a fossil of a trilobite in it. Trilobites are animals which lived long ago. No trilobites are alive now. We would not know about trilobites if there were no fossils in rocks.

Big pieces of trees sometimes turn to rock. All the little holes in the wood fill in with minerals when it turns to rock. Petrified wood tells people where big forests once were.

Layers of water-made rock tell where seas once were.

It is fun to read stories in rocks.

SCIENTISTS NAME ROCKS

To be sure of the names of rocks, scientists do these things.

They break rocks open to see the inside. They smell rocks when they are wet. They feel rocks. They scratch rocks to see how hard they are. They taste rocks. They test rocks with chemicals. They look at them through a hand lens.

It is easy to find rocks
in a woods. There are rocks
in streams, too. A rock needs
to be broken to see it well.
  Each rock should be named.
The name can be put on a piece
of tape and the tape put on
the rock. To learn about rocks:
look at them carefully,
read about them in books,
visit a museum,
         ask a scientist for help.

1. SANDSTONE
2. LIMESTONE
3. SHALE
4. SLATE
5. CONGLOMERATE
6. QUARTZ

SERPENTINE

BRECCIA

It is fun to gather many kinds of rocks.

METAMORPHIC ROCK

WHITE CRYSTAL CALCITE

46

IRON PYRITE

GRANITE PEBBLE

AMETHYST QUARTZ

GARNET CRYSTALS

FELDSPAR CRYSTAL

IMPORTANT THINGS TO KNOW ABOUT ROCKS

Rocks are different sizes.
Rocks are different colors.
Rocks are made in different ways.
Rocks are made under ground.
Rocks are made on top of the ground.
Rocks are made under water.
Rocks are being made all the time.
Rocks are made of minerals.
Each kind of crystal has its own shape.
Some rocks are harder than others.
Rocks are very old.
Some are older than others.
Rocks tell stories of long ago.
Rocks are useful to people.
It is not easy to be sure of
the name of a rock.
There are many kinds of rocks.
Only a few kinds of rocks are in this book.